Contents

> *NOTE:*
> *For the purposes of this book, 1 pint is approximately 500
> millilitres* (ml), *2 pints one litre, and 1 ounce* (oz) *25 grams* (g).

Acknowledgments

The photographs of cookers on pages 32 and 33 are by courtesy of
East Midlands Gas and Creda Electric Ltd.
The photographs on pages 6, 7, 42, 43 (top), 45, 46, 47,
48, 49, 50, 51, 53 are by Tim Clark.

cooking
with
mother

by LYNNE PEEBLES
photographs by JOHN MOYES
and illustrations by ROGER HALL

Ladybird Books Loughborough

This book is all about food
and how to cook,
but before you start
here are some simple rules.

ALWAYS wash your hands
and wear an apron

ALWAYS read the recipe right through
so that you know
exactly what you are doing

ALWAYS be safe: a grown-up *must* be
with you when you cook

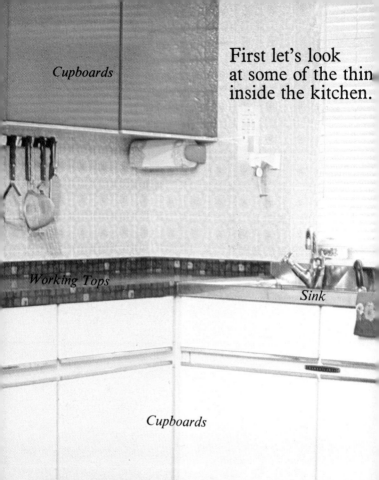

First let's look at some of the thin inside the kitchen.

Cupboards

Working Tops

Sink

Cupboards

6

Refrigerator

Cooker

7

Now collect
all the utensils you need
before you begin.

Here are some of the things
you will be using
and how they are used.

How many of these can you find in your kitchen?

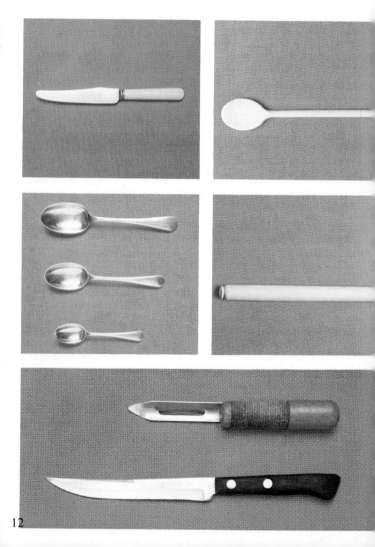

ALWAYS MEASURE CAREFULLY

Count out the things you will need

Using a spoon

*A rounded tablespoon is generally taken to represent 25 g or 1 oz.
Where a level tablespoon is mentioned in a recipe, use a knife as
shown below to level off a heaped tablespoon.*

MORE WAYS TO MEASURE

Fats — butter, margarine, lard

Liquid — milk, water, fruit juices

When an average pack (227 g or 8 oz) of butter, margarine or lard is divided into eight, each portion may be taken to weigh approximately 25 g (1 oz).

THE FOODS WE EAT

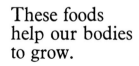

These foods
help our bodies
to grow.

These foods help
to keep us healthy.

These foods give us
lots of energy.

Foods for growth

Foods for energy   Foods for health

At breakfast

HOW YOU MAY EAT THESE FOODS

At tea

At lunch

At supper

DRINKS YOU MAY HAVE
Which is your favourite?

24

NOW — LET'S COOK

but first — those rules again.

Wash your hands and put on an apron.

Read the recipe right through carefully.

Put your pets out of the kitchen when you are going to cook. They may carry germs which could get into your food.

Never lick your fingers
when you are cooking.

ARE YOU SAFE —
is there a grown-up with you?

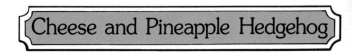

Cheese and Pineapple Hedgehog

THINGS YOU NEED

1 orange
25 cocktail sticks
250 g (10 oz) Cheddar cheese
Small tin of pineapple pieces
1 cherry cut in half
1 small sharp knife
2 plates
Flat dish for serving

THINGS TO DO

1 Wash your hands and
   put on an apron. Wipe
   down the table on which
   you will be working.

2 Cut a slice off one side
   of the orange (so that it
   will stand firmly), and
   place orange cut side
   down on serving plate.

3 Making a bridge with your fingers, cut the cheese in half, then in half again. Now cut each piece into 8.

4 Stick a cocktail stick through each piece of cheese. (Watch out — these sticks are sharp!)

5 Add a piece of pineapple.

6 Break a cocktail stick in half, push one piece through each half cherry, and place at one end of orange to make eyes.

7 Carefully push the sticks of cheese and pineapple into the orange to make the hedgehog spikes.

8 Clear away and wash up.

knives are sharp — be very careful!

THINGS YOU NEED

A few grapes
1 apple

1 banana
Small tin of oranges
or pineapple

1 pear
A few cherries
1 cup of water
A little fruit squash

1 small sharp knife
1 vegetable peeler
1 teaspoon
1 tin opener
Serving dish
1 wooden spoon

THINGS TO DO

1 Wash your hands
  and put on an apron.

2 Open tin of fruit
  and pour into dish.

3 Make a cup of fruit squash
  and pour into dish.

4 Cut cherries in half,
  remove stones, and put
  cherries in dish.

5 Wash grapes, cut in half,
  take out pips, and place
  grapes in dish.

6 Wash apple. Making a
  bridge with your fingers,
  cut apple into four.

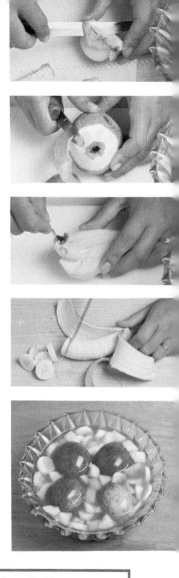

7 Take out core, place slices in dish.

8 Peel pear with vegetable peeler. Cut in half lengthways.

9 Take out core, using a teaspoon. Slice pear and place in dish.

10 Peel banana, cut into slices, add to dish.

11 Stir well so that all the fruit is covered in syrup. Keep in a cool place.

12 Stack all the dirty things on the side of the sink. Wipe table and wash up.

knives again — careful!

Here is a gas cooker.

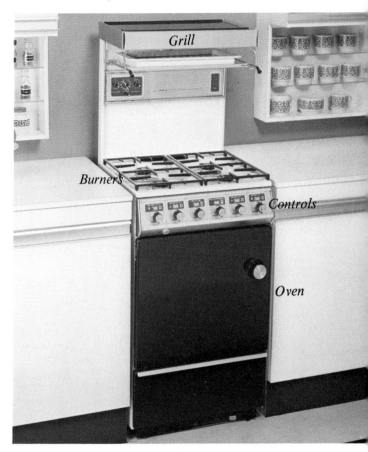

A cooker of any kind can become
very hot and burn you.

Here is an electric cooker.

Controls

Rings

Grill

Oven

**ALWAYS have a grown-up
with you when you use the cooker**

33

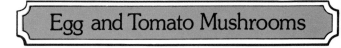
Egg and Tomato Mushrooms

(for 2 people)

THINGS YOU NEED

2 eggs
A few lettuce leaves
1 tomato
Serving dish

1 table knife
1 small sharp knife
1 small pan

THINGS TO DO

1 Wash your hands and put on an apron.

2 Put eggs in pan, cover with cold water, and put
  pan on cooking ring. Turn on heat. When water
  bubbles and boils, time eggs for ten minutes.
  At the end of ten minutes, empty hot water from
  pan, fill pan with cold water, and leave to cool.
  Eggs will then be hardboiled.

> **don't forget — that pan is hot!**

3 While waiting for eggs, wash lettuce leaves.
  Shake dry and arrange in serving dish.

4 Slice tomato into three (you will need the two end pieces).

5 Take out seeds from tomato to leave two hollow shells.

6 When eggs are cool, tap gently on a hard surface and peel off shells carefully.

7 Cut a small piece off one end of each egg. Place eggs on top of lettuce leaves cut side down.

8 Put tomato shell lid on, and serve.

(If liked, the slice of egg can be cut up into small pieces and used to make dots.)

Chocolate Crunchies

THINGS YOU NEED

1 rounded tablespoonful sugar (25 g or 1 oz)
1 rounded tablespoonful cocoa (25 g or 1 oz)
(or 8 squares chocolate)
2 cups Kellogg's Rice Krispies (or Cornflakes)
50 g (2 oz) margarine
1 rounded tablespoonful golden syrup
12 cake cases
Mixing bowl
1 tablespoon
1 wooden spoon
1 small pan

THINGS TO DO

1 Wash your hands and put on an apron.

2 Spread cake cases out on a work top.

3 Put Rice Krispies into mixing bowl. Place margarine, sugar and golden syrup in the pan, place on top of the cooker and heat *very gently*, stirring with wooden spoon until the margarine, sugar and golden syrup have melted together. Remove from heat.

4 Add cocoa (or chocolate) to pan, and mix well.

5 Pour melted mixture into Rice Krispies, and stir gently until they are all coated. When pan is empty, fill it with cold water.

6 Put a tablespoonful into each cake case, then leave them in a cool place to set.

7 Clear away and wash up. Wash pan last of all.

Cheese and Potato Pie

(for 4 people)

THINGS YOU NEED

Large packet of instant potato (500 ml or 1 pint size)
6 rounded tablespoonfuls (150 g or 6 oz) grated
Cheddar cheese
1 tomato
25 g (1 oz) margarine
Ovenproof serving dish
1 fork
1 sharp knife
1 table knife

THINGS TO DO

1 Put on oven at Gas Mark 4
  (electricity 350°F/180°C).

2 Wash your hands and put on an apron.

3 Measure 500 ml (1 pint) of water, pour into pan.
  Place on cooker and bring to boil.

4 Put instant potato in mixing bowl, with
  margarine. When water boils, carefully pour it
  onto potato powder, then mix with fork.

5 Add 4 tablespoonfuls of grated cheese to the potato and mix well. Place potato mixture in serving dish and smooth top with knife.

6 Sprinkle on remaining cheese. Place pie in oven for 20 minutes. (If pie is required at once, however, it can be placed under a hot grill until cheese melts and bubbles.)

7 Cut tomato into quarters and place on top just before serving. A piece of watercress in each corner also makes this dish look attractive.

SAFETY AGAIN ! Bend your knees and not your back when you put things into, and take them out of, the oven

Cherry Tops

THINGS YOU NEED

2 rounded tablespoonfuls sugar (50 g or 2 oz)
50 g (2 oz) margarine
1 egg
2 rounded tablespoonfuls self-raising flour
(50 g or 2 oz)
5 cherries

10 paper cake cases	Bun tins
Mixing bowl	1 table knife
1 wooden spoon	2 teaspoons
1 tablespoon	Serving plate
1 small basin	1 sieve

THINGS TO DO

1 Put on oven at Gas Mark 5
   (electricity 375°F/190°C).

2 Wash your hands and put on an apron.

3 Cut the cherries in half.

4 Put margarine and sugar in mixing bowl, add
   sifted flour.

5 Crack the egg into the small bowl (just to make
   sure it is fresh), then add to the things in the
   mixing bowl.

6 Mix everything (they are called the *ingredients*)
   together with a wooden spoon, until smooth
   and creamy.

7 Put a teaspoonful of mixture into each cake case.

8 Place the bun tray carefully in the oven, and bake the cakes for 15 minutes. When the cakes are cooked, they will be golden brown and firm.

9 Remove cases from bun tray, top each cake with half of a cherry, and leave to cool.

Banana Milk Shake

THINGS YOU NEED

1 banana
2 scoops of icecream
500 ml (1 pint) milk
1 rounded tablespoonful
(25 g or 1 oz) of sugar

2 glasses
1 fork
Mixing bowl
1 whisk

THINGS TO DO

1 Wash your hands
   and put on an apron.

2 Peel banana, put in bowl
   and mash with the fork.

3 Add sugar and milk, and
   whisk until frothy.

4 Pour into glasses, top
   with a scoop of icecream,
   and drink at once.

SALADS
FOR SUMMER

FOR WINTER

THINGS YOU NEED

1 lettuce
4 tomatoes
½ box cress
¼ cucumber
1 bunch spring onions
4 carrots
Grater
Watercress (if liked)
Serving dish
Small sharp knife

THINGS TO DO

1 Wash your hands
   and put on an apron.

2 Tear lettuce leaves
   (do not cut) and
   wash in cold water.

3 Slice tomatoes
   (or make into water
   lilies as shown).

4 Cut and wash cress.

5 Slice cucumber carefully.

6 Cut off root and top of spring onions.

7 Scrub and grate carrots.

CAREFUL WHEN GRATING —
keep your fingers *away* from the grater

---

8 Arrange carefully on a dish or in a salad bowl
and serve with rolled ham (or sardines or any
type of cold meat that you wish).

THINGS YOU NEED

¼ white (hard) cabbage
2 tablespoonfuls (50g or 2oz) sultanas or raisins
1 tablespoonful (25g or 1oz) walnuts
4 carrots

2 apples (red or green)
1 tablespoonful lemon juice
Large bowl
Small sharp knife
Grater

THINGS TO DO

1 Wash your hands and put on an apron.

2 Wash cabbage and chop finely.

3 Wash raisins.

4 Chop walnuts roughly.

5 Scrub and grate carrots.

6 Wash apples,
cut into quarters,

take out core
and chop up
quarters.

7 Sprinkle lemon juice on apple, so that it does not
turn brown.

8 Place prepared ingredients in a bowl, mix·well
and serve with corned beef and boiled egg
(or any other cold meat you like).

WAYS TO HELP IN THE KITCHEN

There are lots of ways you can help
in the kitchen, as well as
with the cooking.

You could help with the washing-up.

And of course tidying-up is most important,
especially when you have finished cooking.

You could prepare the vegetables.

You could set the table.

Ladybird Cake

Mother will make the cake and you can ice it

Cake Make up double the recipe for Cherry Tops
omitting cherries and flavouring the mixture
with 2 teaspoonfuls of cocoa dissolved in
2 tablespoonfuls of warm water. Divide mixture
between two 18 cm (7 in) tins and bake for
20–25 minutes until well risen and firm.
Turn onto cooling rack and leave until cold.

Chocolate butter icing

THINGS YOU NEED

150 g (6 oz) icing sugar
75 g (3 oz) margarine
*2 teaspoonfuls of cocoa dissolved in 1 tablespoonful
warm water*
10 Smarties or cherries

THINGS TO DO

1 Wash your hands and put on an apron.

2 Place all ingredients in a bowl and beat well
   until smooth.

Cut one cake as shown.

4 Spread half of the icing on the uncut cake, and place second cake on top.

5 Decorate with remaining icing and red and yellow Smarties (or cherries cut in half).